T0166339

LAURA BROADBENT

IN ON THE GREAT JOKE

Coach House Books, Toronto

copyright © Laura Broadbent, 2016

first edition

Published with the generous assistance of the Canada Council for the Arts and the Ontario Arts Council. Coach House Books also acknowledges the support of the Government of Canada through the Canada Book Fund and the Government of Ontario through the Ontario Book Fund.

LIBRARY AND ARCHIVES CANADA CATALOGUING IN PUBLICATION
Broadbent, Laura, author
    In on the great joke / Laura Broadbent.

Poems.
ISBN 978-1-55245-336-0

    I. Title.

PS8603.R61I56 2016   C811'.6   C2016-904403-3

In on the Great Joke is available as an ebook: ISBN 978-1-77056-486-2 (EPUB), ISBN 978-1-77056-487-9 (PDF), ISBN 978-1-77056-488-6 (MOBI).

Purchase of the print version of this book entitles you to a free digital copy. To claim your ebook of this title, please email sales@chbooks.com with proof of purchase or visit chbooks.com/digital. (Coach House Books reserves the right to terminate the free digital download offer at any time.)

THE
GREAT
JOKE

This book is dedicated to the memory of Katherine Peacock.

1
WEI WU WEI / DO NOT DO / TAO NOT TAO

' ... as the Situationists said of Sartre turning down the Nobel:
it is not enough to refuse, one should have done nothing to
have merited it in the first place.'

– McKenzie Wark

'Right words sound wrong,' says the Tao Te Ching – or Lao Tzu. People are not sure Lao Tzu existed. If he did, apparently he was born a very old man with a long beard, with long ears, who went on to be two hundred years older than the old man he already was when he was born. Perhaps it makes sense that he who was born in this extraordinary way wrote the *Tao Te Ching*, and, so the story goes, wrote it begrudgingly.

From a Taoist perspective, both language and conventional wisdom are inherently biased and artificial, which is why he says 'the right words sound wrong.' Ursula Le Guin suggests in her translation of the *Tao Te Ching*, 'What you know without knowing you know it is the right kind of knowledge. Any other kind (conviction, theory, dogmatic belief, opinion) isn't the right kind, and if you don't know that, you'll lose the Way.' Because language so easily produces theory, conviction and dogmatic belief, Lao Tzu had to work within language to get out of language. No wonder he wrote begrudgingly. He knew that language is a limited system, and he knew that using this system to write the unwritable meant pandering to the basic human demand for a systematic and empirical explication of all things no matter how mysterious – a demand from which he advised us to be free. So he wrote in verse.

I like to imagine how Lao Tzu would function within contemporary Western culture, how he would gently exploit the rigid systems that articulate our institutions. What if Lao Tzu applied for a teaching position at a university? Subject any such bureaucratic North American institution to Taoist principles and the University – the University that takes itself very seriously – seems based on excessively structured, hierarchical arbitrariness.

There are more than 170 English translations of the *Tao Te Ching*, each of which differently translates the *first line* about it not being translatable. Lao Tzu's begrudging attitude is immediately made clear: the first line is about how futile this naming business is, since the Way cannot be named, and if it could be named it would not be the Way, but if it must be named, it is named Unnameable. Most translations of the *Tao Te Ching* are accompanied by commentary, and these commentaries take great pains to talk about about how the Way cannot be talked about. Just as I am talking about it now. This is part of the Great Joke.

'Turn your thoughts this way and you'll see it's just swagger
and bluster and not firm belief.'

– Lucretius

These are the machinations
of one of the world's ragged
human minds which is nothing
oh nothing
like the silent
and knowing Tao.

Practice not-doing,
And everything will fall into place.

Even in the isolated moments
of euphonious connection,
I hear the thin howl of its decay.
The wind howls through him,
through his shoddy insulation.
I can't not hear it, can't not
hear it. All. The. Time. Hear. It.

Things arise and she lets them.
Things disappear and she lets them.

'The Animals aren't going to come.
They never will, they aren't going to.
Even if you live forever.'
'Yeah, but everything is 50 percent off, so … '

Darkness within darkness.
The gateway to all understanding.

The slight woman tepidly eating her salad
considers the whole world deeply impolite.
Chewing is the most indecent to her of all
and she is still not over
animal mastication.
She horrifies herself by practising it publicly.
'Oh my God,' she thinks, stiffly placing
an olive in her mouth. 'Holy motherfucking
God Lord Jesus,' staring dead-straight ahead.

She has but doesn't possess,
Acts but doesn't expect.

The mistake of glancing at a window
that reflects us walking side by side –
the vision a veil flickering
with the fragility of the moment –
blink wrong and it's gone. Ta-da!

When her work is done, she forgets it.
That is why it lasts forever.

'What were you wearing?'
'Like … a dress.'

If you overvalue possessions,
People begin to steal.

After all the trouble,
be more like trees.

However splendid the views,
She stays serenely in herself.

Denial and repression
represent our chief
creative forces.
Create a shrine to them,
leave offerings of
incense and Gatorade.

It is like an eternal void:
Filled with infinite possibilities.

Keep speaking
in another language
so I don't hear.
Just stand there
and look good.
I love that, baby.

The more you use it, the more it produces;
The more you talk about it, the less you understand.

I've been trying to raise the bar higher than
'Don't make terrible mistakes' for thirty years.
Yes, but do you make deft mistakes?
Yes, but do you make dexterous mistakes?

Hold on to the centre.

The simple goal to love him
perfectly is impossible.
Or to keep him.
Forget men, men are of the moment,
the moment which is water.
The trembling reflected moment
of walking side by side – there he is
and then I blink heavily
and the reflection shatters.

Because she has let go of herself,
She is perfectly fulfilled.

The story proceeds as thus:
the starved child is presented
with the toy of her heart's desire;
let her touch it, play with it,
treat it as her own. Let her
slow-glow with gentle pride,
then take it from her.
Say to her accusingly,
'This is not yours, nothing
in this world is yours, ever.'

Chase after money and security
And your heart will never unclench.

'Meanwhile there are the stars, and they make no sense.'

Can you coax your mind from its wandering
And keep to the original oneness?

Where is the comfortable home,
where is the place to unbend?
Groundlessness. That's the [no]where,
it's groundlessness. 'Fuck, really?
Couldn't it be in, like, Oakland?'

Can you cleanse your inner vision
Until you see nothing but light?

How many nice objects do you have?
Yeah, but are they really nice?
I tried on a blazer I quite liked
while the air continued to fill
with poison at a relaxed pace.

Can you step back from your own mind
And thus understand all things?

The idea was that love is holy,
but Drew said, 'No, it's doughnuts, LB,
it's doughnuts, doughnuts that are holy,
kid, it's doughnuts. I can eat twelve
in a row, easily, if I'm feeling
kind of emotional, or maybe,
maybe celebrating something.'
The heart is able to hold so much
because of its holes.

We work with being,
But non-being, is.

'This page is intentionally left blank.'

When you stand with your own two feet,
You will always keep your balance.

'How would you feel if you were colonized by China?'
'Aroused.'

Above, it isn't bright.
Below, it isn't dark.

'I hope the terrifying God
of Poetry fucks your face
and you cry tears of reality.'

Just realize where you came from:
This is the essence of wisdom.

Listen, I'm going to give you the best I've got,
and eventually, it will not be enough.
Still, the moments with you are really good,
even though they're as good as dead.
How lucky I am to live good as dead
moments with you, for you are quality.
You are a quality corpse, you know that?

Thus the master travels all day
Without leaving home.

'Can you tell me what my value is?'
(This was mistake number one.)

Do you have the patience to wait
Till your mud settles and the water clears?

'A man's penis. Nearby.'
'Really?'
'Yes –
a man's penis, nearby.'

Can you remain unmoving
Till the right action arises by itself?

When you tell me tales,
the curtains of your chest part
and I watch your childhood
stagger across the stage,
all the taut traumas ticking away,
forming this person in front of me,
who makes such excellent Jokes.

The ancient masters were profound and subtle.
Their wisdom, unfathomable.

Behold the light in the eyes
of the nicest man in the world:
it is fear! the driving force!
Oh my God, SO not the Way.

Watch the turmoil of beings,
But contemplate their return.

Night is personal
and relentless.
I lived the story
and not even I
can sort it out.
What a fugue.

If you don't realize the source,
You stumble in confusion and sorrow.

Have you wanted to lift your hands
and let the wind sweep you away
like an abandoned birthday balloon
becoming smaller and smaller
in a too-blue sky as an after-effect
of remembering? Envy of escaped
helium balloons is called Balloon Envy.
'You're falling apart.'
'Yes, this seems to be the case. Yes.'

If you don't trust the people,
You make them untrustworthy.

How life is set right at the sight
of two old ladies looking at art books.
One lady with very useful pockets
in her white cargo pants moves
like her body is composed of twigs
fastened together with smaller twigs.

The master doesn't talk, he acts.
When his work is done,
The people say, 'Amazing:
We did it, all by ourselves!'

Play tricks of perspective. Think of space
so vast it hurts your mind – just something to do.
In my downtime, I play a game called Dissolve My Ego
in which the idea of space is so vast it kills the mind.
Or, conceive of the rest of the world not knowing
or caring about the people who vex your mind most.
Conceive of the dead and conceive
of what vexed them to death, conceive of them conceiving
of future you and having no idea what will vex you to the grave.
Imagine Jean Rhys sitting alone at a café, with all of her vexations.
And so on. App developers, inquire within.

I alone am expressionless,
Like an infant before it can smile.

A mother with a bountiful ass
chases her toddler who runs,
maniacally, toward the busy street,
his arms raised in suicidal delight,
the mother's ass moving in all directions at once
as she runs and grabs the lifted arm so violently
he hovers and dangles at an odd angle
and for a moment we can see
how the mother wants to kill the child
she just rescued from being killed.
How does the heart even.

Let's just take a moment
to honour the Great Joke.
Is this an allegory?
Absolutely nothing makes sense.
Except laughter, evil laughter and Borges.
Vexations of the heart, mind, whatever,
are toddlers compelling you
to run into traffic.
Now yank your mind up by its chubby little arm
and regret ever having it in the first place.

I am different from ordinary people.
I drink from the Great Mother's breasts.

He explains I am not crazy but traumatized
and my coping mechanisms are broken.
Pretty much any coping mechanism is broken
and I wonder, what does a human do
that isn't a coping mechanism?
Sina said never give your whole heart
to anybody. Never even occurred to me.

How can it make her radiant?
Because she lets it.

While the funeral pyre, while the ash,
while the grandfathers wobble,
I fold my laundry, sweep the floor,
I plan my diet, I close my doors.

Be like the forces of nature:
When it blows, there is only wind.

Whatever is behind the eyes,
looking through the eyes,
looking out from the skull,
looking out from the face,
is saying let me out, let me out
for the time being but then again
I might need back in.

For lack of a better name,
I call it the Tao.

The always yearning
to be above or below
the human realm, just not in it,
just not subject to it.

What she desires is non-desire
What she learns is to unlearn.

Don't call a psychiatrist
but I've been ready to go
ever since I didn't arrive.
When people look at me, smug
or strengthened by their opinions,
I imagine spontaneously dissolving
into a pile of ash and asking,
'Does the reality of who I am

match your evaluation? Besides,
your Ray-Bans hide nothing.'

A good traveller has no fixed plans
And is not intent upon arriving.

The idea of becoming successful,
in any worldly way whatsoever,
is as real as any Hollywood movie.
All I have ever wanted
is to be who I am,
and I am doing it.

Know the male,
Yet keep to the female.

The request as prayer is always
'Take me away. Take me away.'
It bubbles multiple times a day
and has for the past thirty years.
'Hi! How are you?'
'Hi! Fine! You?'

Know the personal
Yet keep to the impersonal.

With the tired, exasperated,
onward look of a mother,
she watches our little men
tramp along out of their minds
with testosterone and blow shit up.

The master lets them go their own way
And resides at the centre of the circle.

'But she's too good-looking to have bad luck!'
My witticisms that are easy and put others
at ease have now successfully committed suicide.

Weapons are the tools of violence;
All decent men detest them.

What do you like on your toast?
Mondays: alienation + dislocation.
Tuesdays: loss + trauma.
Soon it will occur to us to cull
and trade tales of our various anorexias.
Do not be that bitter lady who lives only
on her hatred for a man who has long ago
forgotten her. That song's been sung.
Sung-sung. Eat your toast.

If you stay in the centre and embrace death
With your whole heart, you will endure forever.

Don't worry, I realize you are just a body
failing to make itself understood. Despite
what they say, I come bearing the goods:
you do not have to be functioning all the time.

She perceives the universal harmony, even amid great pain,
Because she has found peace in her heart.

The songs of marching bands,
slightly off-key,
are the perfect soundtrack
to the mockery of all things.
Subsequently, 'This is That'
is a phrase I attempt
to understand.
I am the marching band and
I am what the marching band
perfectly mocks, off key.
*A tuba moans, three cymbals
crash off the beat, out of sync.*

LAO TZU APPLIES FOR A UNIVERSITY
TEACHING POSITION

To whom it may concern (it is my hope that no one is concerned):

The class I do not propose to not-teach is called 'Wei Wu Wei,' Do Not Do, or alternately called 'Nothing Much.' The nature of the course is for students to practice the skills of being '*su*' – simple, plain, like raw silk, and '*p'u*' – natural and honest, like uncut wood.

Your institution is well-known to be a place of Higher Education so, naturally, in the course of the course, the students will seek to occupy the lowest place possible. If they are a place they are the lowest place, if they are a taste, they are a flat, tasteless Nothing Much.

In the spirit of Wei Wu Wei, I teach without teaching. For the first class, I am twenty miles away, gazing elsewhere.

It is not possible to explain what it is to teach without teaching, or what it is to teach without teaching the concept of Do Not Do.

I can say this: sometimes I will come to class with a clay pot; the lesson is called 'Where the Pot is Not.' It is said you can double the size of the universe by understanding where the pot is not. Hollowed-out clay is where the pot is not and where the pot is not is where it is most useful.

My syllabus says this and this only: 'Need little, want less, forget the rules, be untroubled.'

Some students believe Wei Wu Wei is an easy credit. This is the belief of the ever-wanting soul who sees only what it wants to see. They do not understand what self-discipline is required to align themselves with the Way, rather than with their own nature. Wei Wu Wei is counter-intuitive and counter-institutional. It takes a great effort to achieve effortlessness and it often takes the entire semester for the students to merely comprehend that they do not comprehend effortlessness. The Way is paradoxical and paradoxes allow us to apprehend the mystery of which we are part.

It is neither correct nor incorrect to say that Wei Wu Wei is a finishing school for death – how to die without resistance, how to enter the stream, to flow.

The end of the course is 'Understanding the Corpse' – that is, to understand that the body comes to its ending, but there is nothing to fear, endings occur but something endures, and what endures is the Way. To be sure, be pliant and supple while alive, as stiffness and strictness are for the dead.

For the lesson 'To Bear and Not to Own,' I assign complicated, time-intensive papers. On the due date of the Great Papers, I ask the students to hand their papers to the right. The person to the right is to erase the name and replace it with their own, and it is for that paper they shall receive the grade. I tell them this will double the size of the universe.

Not praising the praiseworthy keeps people uncompetitive. This exercise is not to cherish altruism, which is merely the other side of egoism. Students learn, like nature, to be selfless, absent of positive ethical or political values. When the self is let go all that is left is what the soul needs.

The successful students, the unwanting souls who rid themselves of their grades, will see what is hidden, while the unsuccessful students, the ever-wanting souls who do not part with their grades, will see only what they want. To do good, work well, lie low.

The pedagogical non-approach of Wei Wu Wei angers university students who demand a certain type of exact instruction, which is all university students. In accordance with their desires, I assign very complicated texts; the texts however, have nothing to do with the class.

At the end of each week, I hand out marks which the students are free to trade with each other. If those with high marks are willing to trade with those with low marks, or if those with low marks are content with their low marks and content with others having high marks, or if those with the high marks do not relate to their high marks and regard those with low marks as high-markers, the class is well on the Way. This is the mysterious power.

Of student absences, I accept excuses such as 'I took a very long walk' or 'I was sweeping my floor' or 'I was on my way then I went another way' or 'I did not leave my room since it's the inner eye that really sees the world.'

The end-of-term assessment is as follows: Is the student always alert like a cat's ears? Is the student always polite and quiet like a butler? Is the student always elusive like mist? Is the student always blank like fresh snow? Is the student always empty like where the pot is not?

Effortlessly,
Lao Tzu

A MEDITATION ON TRANSLATION, OR: TWENTY-ONE
TRANSLATIONS OF THE FIRST STANZA OF THE *TAO TE
CHING*, WITH TWENTY-ONE COMMENTS UPON THE
TRANSLATIONS

'I am not interested in other words for honey. I am interested
in honey.'

– Sina Queyras

1

The way you can go
Isn't the real way.
The name you can say
Isn't the real name.
    – Le Guin

Go whichever way you want.
On your way you are either with the Way
or on your way you are without the Way.
Either way you make your way.

2

The Way that can be described
is not the absolute Way;
the name that can be given
is not the absolute name.
    – Beck

A hose by any other name
would absolutely spray as sweet.
Trust those you know who have
absolutely changed their name.

3

There are ways
but the Way is uncharted.
There are names
but not nature in words.
    – Blakney

There are words but words
get in the way.
Don't tell her you love
her, love her.

4

Existence is beyond
the power of words to define:
Terms may be used
but are none of them absolute.
    – Bynner

Do you see words as though words
are meanings? Words lead away
from the Way unless they point every
which way, which is annoying.

5

The Tao that can be described
is not the eternal Tao.
The name that can be spoken
is not the eternal Name.
    – Byrn

The Tao is the equivalent
of good, crisp drugs.
Sex-positive and full
of jokes, god-sanctioned.

6

A way can be a guide,
but not a fixed path;
names can be given,
but not permanent labels.
　　– Cleary

The Tao is invisible, unsayable, elusive,
which is not to say it's outside you
since the Tao is most like water
and even you are 70 percent without trying.

7

To guide what can be guided
is not constant guiding.
To name what can be named
is not constant naming.
　　– Hansen

The Tao is not unlike flatulence,
present, but unseen.
A Taoist fart should breed
a lightness of heart, easy love.

8

The Tao that can be told
is not the invariant Tao;
the names that can be named
are not the invariant Names.
    – LaFargue

There are thirteen ways
of looking at the Tao
and each one is one
with the blackbird.

9

The Tao that can be trodden
is not the enduring and unchanging Tao.
The name that can be named
is not the enduring and unchanging name.
    – Legge

Emotions are in the Tao, emotions
are not of the Tao, they make you
think things mean things. They're okay.
Maybe don't believe in them so much.

10

A Tao that one can Tao
is not the entire Tao.
A name that one can name
is not the entire name.
    – Lindauer

A Taco that one can Taco
is not the entire Taco,
a game that one can game
is not the entire game.

11

> *The Tao that can be told of*
> *is not the Absolute Tao.*
> *The Names that can be given*
> *are not Absolute Names.*
>   – Lin Yutang

Amongst people,
extroverts feel one with the Tao.
Amongst not-people.
introverts feel one with the Tao.

12

> *The way that can be told of*
> *is hardly an eternal, absolute, unvarying one.*
> *The name that can be coded and given*
> *is no absolute name.*
>   – McDonald

'Knock, Knock!'
'Who's there?'
'Tao.'
'Tao who?'
' ... '

13

The Way that can be experienced
is not true;
the world that can be constructed
is not real.
　　　– Merel

Imperceptibility, indiscernibility
and impersonality – the three virtues.
A univocal ontology: all beings express
their being with a single voice.

14

The Tao that can be told
is not the eternal Tao.
The name that can be named
is not the eternal Name.
　　　– Mitchell

To hold fast to your beliefs
as though they encompass reality
is a sad arrogance,
says Ursula K. Le Guin.

15

The Tao that can be followed
is not the eternal Tao.
The name that can be named
is not the eternal name.
　　　– Muller

In order to create,
you must lose your identity,
you must disappear,
you must become unknown.

16

The way that becomes a way
is not the Immortal Way.
The name that becomes a name
is not the Immortal Name
  – Red Pine

Some follow the Dow.
Others, the Tao.
While neither makes sense
only one makes No Sense.

17

The Tao that can be expressed
is not the eternal Tao.
The name that can be defined
is not the unchanging name.
  – Ta-Kao

Q: What do you call
a Dadaist who is
one with the Tao?
A: Taotaoist.

18

Tao is beyond words
and beyond understanding.
Words may be used to speak of it,
but they cannot contain it.
　　– Walker

If we raise our boys to be like water,
soft and yielding, but strong enough
to wear away mountains, our girls
will have to learn to love the nice guy.

19

The principle that can be enunciated
is not the one that always was.
The being that can be named
is not the one that was at all times.
　　– Wieger

All the books are full
of people naming it,
a horse of changing colours,
blue, red, puce and so on.

20

The infinity that can be conceived
is not the everlasting Infinity.
The infinity that can be described
is not the perpetual Infinity.
　　– World

Not conceived, but intuited.
Effective music intuits
the everlasting infinity
even though the song ends.

21

Tao can be talked about,
but not the Eternal Tao.
Names can be named,
but not the Eternal name.
    – Wu

The follower of the Way
has no weapons, she opens
her empty hands and says
to the enemy, 'You win.'

SHORT FILM

CHARACTERS

Max: Tall, paunchy, in his early thirties.
Girl: Tall, slim, pretty, in her early twenties.

SCENE ONE

A green hill, a blue sky – candy-green and candy-blue. A white jet stream incises the otherwise empty sky. The entire curve of the hill fits the shot.

A fifteen-second shot of the hill, the sky, the jet stream, the jet sound, the slight wind.

Max appears from the left and begins up the hill, unhurried. He is wearing a red jacket.

When he is midway, a female voice becomes audible. It yells something repeatedly.

The yelling escalates and the girl appears from the left. She is naked.

She is at once marching, running and stumbling.

Her fists are clenched and pump at her sides each time she yells.

She is breathless. It appears she has been following him for many miles.

The girl is calling his name and repeats it in varying intensities: sometimes a shrill 'Max!'; other times a desperate 'Ma-ha-hax'; other times

'Max...' in a tone that pretends it was not shrill or desperate a moment before; then an enraged 'MAX!'

Max does not turn and it is unclear whether he cannot or will not hear her.

He walks down the other side of the hill, keeps an even pace, hands in his pockets.

The naked girl reaches the top of the hill. She trips as she calls to him.

She falls face-first onto the grass.

She gapes at Max's back as he strolls down the hill.

She calls to him.

She remains on the ground, she wails, she rips clumps of grass with each fist, then she goes limp and silent.

The girl's heaving back indicates sobbing.

The young man walks out of the shot.

END SCENE.

SCENE TWO

A midnight hot-tub party in the winter.

There are young and attractive people in the steaming tub.

They have a supercilious air – the hot tub unites them in this.

Max, in his red jacket, leans next to the hot tub with his back toward the camera as he laughs with the attractive people, beer in hand.

A swish-swishing of thighs in snowpants is heard before the girl runs into the shot.

She is wearing a pink one-piece snowsuit.

She grabs at the back of Max's red jacket.

The girl calls his name.

Max jerks free and runs off-screen.

The girl, in her one-piece snowsuit, takes waddling steps in Max's direction, calling once more.

She stops and stares in the direction he has gone.

She has to tilt her head back to see out of her hood.

Her cheeks are pink and her breath is clouds.

She stares after him in this manner for ten seconds.

Her eyes squeeze shut and she sobs as she calls one last time.

The girl pivots and stares at the hut tub full of people who are staring at her.

The only animate things are her frozen breaths and the steam rising from the hot tub.

The girl waddles back toward the hot tub, yanks a beer from a blond girl's hand, smashes it on the side of the tub and holds it close to the face of the blond girl, who is stricken.

The girl drops the bottle and swishes away.

END SCENE.

SCENE THREE

A busy downtown street at noon.

The camera remains still as crowds stream and bob by.

Most of the people are walking away from the camera.

A man in a red coat is among the crowd that walks past.

He is about thirty strides ahead when a girl runs after him.

It is clear the girl has called something but there is no sound in this scene.

The man turns. It is not Max.

END SCENE.

END FILM.

2
INTERVIEWS

WHAT A RELIEF NOT TO MEET YOU IN PERSON: AN HOMAGE TO THE ALCHEMY OF READING

'Readers like this one undoubtedly have creative potential. And this implies that reading my fiction requires a certain creativity. This particular way of reading has to be more than just gazing at the accepted meanings of the text on a literal level, because you are reading messages sent out by the soul, and your reading is awakening your soul into communication with the author's. Contact between souls is possible; that is my conviction.'

– Can Xue, 'A Short Piece on Experimental Fiction'

An everyday act of alchemy is that of radical receptivity, radical receptivity being listening, listening, in this case, being reading, reading being collaboration, collaboration being a combination of two or more things to make an entirely new thing, collaboration thus being alchemy if the loose term for alchemy is 'a seemingly magical process of transformation, creation or combination.' Thou art that, this is that, that art thou, that thou art, you are that, that you are. Borders are malleable, consumption alters the consumer's composition, relationships are magnetic. You are what you read. It is easier to comprehend and justify a statement like 'you are what you eat' as opposed to 'you are what you read' (both true) since 'you are what you eat' can be understood through empirically observable chemical processes (a sick fish makes a man shit-piss, fresh figs make a man's shits bliss) while 'you are what you read' can be understood through less obvious subtle metaphysical alchemical processes.

Reading is listening and there is most certainly a dearth of listening, as in really listening. To really listen is a skill in which one must generate acute sensitivity, and an active receptivity. To reiterate, being receptive is not passive, it is active. Being receptive is not 'feminine' (here used pejoratively), it is just intelligent. If you think of the best person you know, I bet that person is a good listener, and the worst person you know is not a good listener, at least not to you. A not-good listener is insensitive and insensitivity is unintelligent since insensitivity lacks scope, while a good listener is by default sensitive, in which case that person is also intelligent since one needs scope in order to be sensitive. A good listener/reader is often an empathetic person and an empathetic person is empathetic because they are able to perform the act of listening with the maximum perspective possible. Perspective comes from what else but a lot of listening, and reading is an alchemical form of listening.

From the outside, reading can seem isolated, antisocial, indulgent, boring or nerdy because the subtle magic is not immediately observable. When you are witnessing someone reading, if they are indeed a skilled listener and not a passive escapist (no judgment toward the joy of the latter), what you are actually witnessing is an intimate act of collaboration and creation, what you are witnessing is a transformation which is also known as magic. Magic can, at its most basic, mean a change that is wonderful and exciting.

Objectively, texts are blocks of words in a certain order. One hundred copies can be made of the same book with the same words in the same order, and we can say, 'These books are the same.' But when the book is enmeshed with a human reader's subjectivity, the words are transformed based on the particular configuration of the receiver's conscious and unconscious structures. Subjectively, a text has many meanings indeed – one book can be one thousand different books if one thousand people read it. Furthermore, let it be said that when a person picks up a book they are choosing to listen as an activity, a powerful decision often overlooked. I see this choice as a very beautiful and elegant thing a human can do, completely devoid of class or any other divisive hierarchy. Seeing people read has never ceased to calm me, because they are choosing to listen, which is a gentle and intelligent and elegant and stylish choice. I am speaking of a certain kind of reading, and if you are reading this you know what kind of reading I mean, I mean reading as contact between souls.

One of the most satisfying things about reading as with the act of creation, is the control. Since one has to render oneself vulnerable in order to be radically receptive, one feels more able or inclined to do so when one still possesses a sense of control; the reader can put down the book at any time, the reader is not pressured to respond to the writer's words as one would in the terrifying and self-conscious context of everyday conversations, and the reader is free to interpret the words in any way he or she chooses, if at all. What a relief that the reader never has to meet the writer in person, a meeting which may be intolerable. From reading her biography and seeing her in interviews, I am sure meeting Clarice Lispector would be traumatizing, yet encountering her writing is manageable though even her writing threatens to be overbearing. There is a bombardment of information through interacting with the living. When one is overwhelmed reading, one can simply close the book and take a moment to recover, or one can sleep on it, all without having to think of a polite way to exit the conversation. Wouldn't it be nice to just put a bookmark in someone?

When reading, an ideal conversation is happening wordlessly between the reader and the 'writer,' as signified by their words, which is ironic considering the medium is words. The writer's words (as a stand-in for the writer herself) have the effect of piercing little holes in one's consciousness in order to let new and oneiric light sluice in – the beginning of the transformation. This potentially violent or euphoric experience occurs in a safe place, in solitude, with all guards down. The sort of conversation that we call reading can be described by the open-minded as spiritual, or at least visceral, in that it feels telepathic, in that far more than words are being transmitted, not just intellectually as is most commonly assumed. The light, too, goes both ways – a writer's words morph when filtered through the light of an individual's consciousness while also bestowing a whole new light upon that consciousness that it may not have had before. This subtly profound transformation has the effect of a fragrance; sensitive readers walk away from books with a sense of the author as an ineffable presence, the affective experience of their words being something far more complex than just words.

The following interviews are an homage to the alchemy of reading. Each author, besides perforating my consciousness and rendering me changed, leaves a fragrance when I put down their books. Of course the fragrance changes from reader to reader. For example, one may say that Sebald stinks while another picks up a hint of herring, sea, wolf piss, steel and balsam fir. The final interview, however, is an interview with an empath about seeing. It just wanted to be there.

Since the authors are dead, I used, for each, one of their books as the only source from which their answers would come; from each book I arranged phrases which I took to be their dominant scents in order to distill their essence. Of course their answers sound like both them and me combined, but that is what happens when one reads, not unlike what happens when one loves – you cannot feel where you begin and the other ends.

'There are always two deaths, the real one and the one people know about.'

– Jean Rhys

When Jean Rhys worked as a chorus girl, her name was Vivienne, or Ella Gray, or Emma. Once, she was the mistress of a wealthy stockbroker named Lancelot. Sometimes she worked as a nude model. Jean Rhys did not have good luck. She married a guy named Willem, then a guy named Leslie, then a guy named Max, who died in jail. She had an affair with a guy named Ford Madox Ford who propelled her writing career, but not enough. Later, Jean Rhys took off to the coast to live in wine-drenched obscurity for many years. She was known to be cantankerous. She once said that no novelist can really be happy over any great length of time, though if she had the choice, she'd prefer to be happy and not write.

You have your heroines compulsively seek salvation through men. What drove this compulsion in your own life?

As if I were following a ritual,
as if my life moved in a circle,
I felt a great desire to please,
to make him look at me kindly.

I wanted to attract and charm him.
I consistently realized
that it might be extremely important
that I should attract and charm him.
To get away, I married.

I was longing to explain,
to say, 'This is how I am. This is.'
I was longing for him to see.

Yet I knew
that if I could get to the end
of what I was,
it would be the truth
about myself, about the world,
about everything
one puzzles and pains about.

*Yet to you, to your heroines, the men always end up being empty signifiers;
rather than being a safe place, they perpetuate a cycle of self-destruction.
Your males are contemptuous of women, they condescend, they silence,
they control, they abandon.*

I was all right
until I met that swine.
But he sort of – I don't know –
he sort of smashed me up.

I often wanted to hit him.
I was possessed with one of the fits of rage
that were becoming part of my character.
I wanted to fly at him, strike him,
but I thought that he would probably
kill me back.

The audience rocks
with laughter

at the exhausted,
collapsing woman.
It's so easy
to make a person
who hasn't got anything
seem wrong.

It's always like that.
When you are tottering,
somebody peculiarly well qualified
comes along and shoves.
Stamps on you.

If I was bound for hell,
let it be hell.
Justice. I've heard that word.
No more false heavens.
No more damned magic.

But in spite of this
my brain kept on labouring,
latching in an anxious fashion
about the men.

After the men fail them, your heroines revolt against the power they have given away, but it is always too late – they have given it away. So their revolt is often a rage against themselves and against these men. The attempted revolt often ends up in a breakdown where they experience one of many inner deaths. You say there are two deaths – the real one, and the one that people see. Is it even possible to describe the former?

I was very tired, as though
I had retired somewhere far off –
the ghost of myself coming out
of the fog to meet me
crouching warily
like an alley cat.

And I felt as if all my life
and all myself
were drifting
like fog. Nothing
to lay hold of –

I was tortured, my brain
was making a huge effort, clawing
to nothingness. Always
in another minute ...
I would know.

At the same time,
in a miraculous manner, some essence
of me was shooting upward like fireworks.
I was great. I was a defiant flame
shooting upward not to plead
but to devour.

I had abandoned myself.
A dam inside my head split,
I leant my head on my arms
and sobbed. I was kneeling
and heaving and wishing

I had brought my other
handkerchief.

Everybody's life was like that.

And suddenly I was immensely calm
and indifferent to anything
that had ever happened
or could possibly happen to me.

And then I felt very cold
and then I felt so tired that
nothing mattered except sleep
where I am empty of everything.

I am empty of everything
but the thin, frail ghosts
in my room.

It was like that.
It was always like that.

After, I sat placidly
with my knees rather wide apart,
and my eyes fixed.

*You disappeared into obscurity for a long while, and your heroines often
experienced exile as well. Is this the natural movement following an inner
death, which is the first death?*

Now I no longer wish to be loved, beautiful, happy or successful.
I want one thing and one thing only – to be alone.
Can I help it if my heart beats, if my hands go cold?
And then the days did come when I was alone. Quite alone.
No voice, no touch, no hand. How long must I lie here? Forever?
No, only for a couple hundred years.
Oh, no place is a place to be sober in.

A black screen. We hear a woman speaking on the telephone. The script may be improvised by the actress but, in essence, should be akin to:

'No. No! I didn't say that! –

'But I didn't mean to, no –

'But I didn't –

'No, please listen –

'All I was trying to say was –

'But you didn't. I had to go alone –

'I was alone there! I –

'You're not mean! I'm just saying it was –

'No! No, that isn't true! Please don't –

'No you're right I didn't want to have it. You didn't force me to –

'I know you were busy, it's okay, I'm just saying –

'But I just wanted you to care about –'

Her agitation escalates with each line until the black screen is replaced by a shot of her in her living room, pacing, repeatedly insisting, 'I am not crazy' until she is, indeed, hysterical. At this point, the audio of her voice fades enough for Werner Herzog to narrate.

HERZOG: 'Behind an innocuous closed door on a quiet street on the west side of Manhattan, a woman ... caught in the throes of her Woman nature has caught our eye ... If we go toward her we ... and the man she speaks to ... are heading toward certain death ... The man on the phone who is challenging her is of course challenging Woman herself. And she hits back ... she just hits back ... that is all ... and that's what is grandiose about her ... and we have to accept that she is much stronger than we are ... Kinsey always says she is full of ... erotic elements ... I don't see her so much as erotic, I see her more ... full of ... obscenity. Woman are ... violent, base. I do not see anything erotical in her ... I see fornication and asphyxiation and choking and ... fighting for survival and growing and just ... rotting away ... Of course she is misery but ... it is the same misery that is all around us ... The trees in Manhattan are in misery and the birds are in misery ... I do not think they sing ... they just screech in pain ... Woman is an unfinished country ... she's still prehistorical ... the only thing that is lacking with her is the dinosaurs ... She is like a curse weighing on an entire landscape ... and whoever goes deep into her has his share of that curse. So we are cursed with what we are doing here ... She is a land that God ... if he exists ... has created in anger ... She is the only land where creation is yet unfinished. Taking a close look at her ... there is some sort of harmony ... and it is the harmony of overwhelming and collective murder ... And we in comparison to the articulate vileness ... and baseness and ... obscenity of Woman ... we in comparison to that enormous articulation ... we only sound and look like badly pronounced and half-finished sentences of a stupid suburban novel ... a cheap novel ... And we have to become humble in front of her overwhelming misery and overwhelming fornication ... overwhelming growth, and overwhelming lack of order ... with her, even the stars in the sky appear a mess ... With her we see there is no harmony in the universe ... .We have to get acquainted with this idea that there is no harmony as we have conceived it ... But when I say this ... I say this full of admiration for Woman ... It is not that I hate her ... I love her ... I love her very much ... But I love her against my better judgment.'

The audio returns to the woman, begging with her interlocutor not to hang up, and still imploring him to understand that she is not crazy. She inquires whether or not he is still present before she hangs up, falls to her

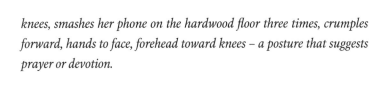

knees, smashes her phone on the hardwood floor three times, crumples forward, hands to face, forehead toward knees – a posture that suggests prayer or devotion.

*Note: the actress for this role should be young, fit and attractive, O blood type, with one to four moles above the waist but none larger than one quarter inch in diameter, with perfect teeth that shimmer like polished ivory, and ample breasts that bespeak a simultaneous *good morning*, *goodnight*, *sleep well* and *sweet dreams*.

A POSTHUMOUS INTERVIEW WITH CLARICE LISPECTOR

'[Lispector is who] Kafka would have been had he been a woman, or if Rilke had been a Jewish Brazilian born in the Ukraine. If Rimbaud had been a mother, if he had reached the age of fifty. If Heidegger could have ceased being German.'

– Hélène Cixous

Clarice Lispector's words violently kick up the fine dust of my dreaming self. She evokes the female id/it/unconscious ... or something. That is, she manages to write the unsayable. She is unleashed, horrifying eroticism and she embraces the ugliest human mess because this is her material and she renders the mess as graceful and natural and pure as a mountain stream, right into the unified field of pure blissful emptiness. Home run.

Can you name a first impulse to write?

A kind of crazy, crazy harmony.
A hallelujah that fuses the darkest
human howl of the pain of separation
but is a shout of diabolical happiness.
The evil that is the good.

I like intensities. Fury of impulses.
It has nothing to do with a job
because I don't earn money with it.
I just wanted to look. I'm going to stop
because it's Saturday.
I just end up knowing what the world is like.

What is this bravery of not following any accepted literary norms or rules?

Nobody holds me,
my demon is an assassin –
doesn't fear punishment –
a life of magic violence –
a genius that governs fire.

When I think of what I've already lived,
it seems to me I was leaving
my bodies all along the way –

I trot back and forth
without boundaries.
Oh, force of all
that exists,
help me.

What is life?

LIFE

IS

SUPER

NATURAL

Pain is exacerbated life.
Coming-into-being is a slow, slow, good pain.
It's a full stretch to the point
that the person can stretch no more.
The process hurts.
And the blood is thankful.

You breathe, you breathe.
The air is it.

It?

It is the instant at which the wheel of the automobile
going at high speed barely touches the ground.
It is the what.
It is the shout of something that shouts and surges forth.
It is all-consuming.
It coils around me and is sexually alive.
It is harshly alive.
It is the great power of potentiality.
It's useless to think about it.
I won't discover it and yet I live off it.
It is because of the lack of answers.
The milk is it.
My life will be very long because each moment is it.
It's a question of time's simultaneity.
It is the eroticism inherent in living things.
It is the liturgy of dissonant swarms of insects that rise from
    pestilent bogs.
It is the evil that dominates me.
It isn't hard and it comes easily.
It's a matter of not fighting it and simply surrendering.
It's melancholy.
It's morning.
It – I feel like calling it the jewel of death.
Telling it would be to betray it.
It is.
It is the real encounter.

It is all living things, man notwithstanding.

And it is a riot of wonderment.

Its perfume is an insane mystery.

It's a flower that impetuously controls its own savagery.

How uncertain it is.

Yet it's within the order.

It is people who are a little ugly and at the same time in harmony.

It is the courage to live.

There is no formula for it.

It is an inexplicable love that makes the heart beat faster.

It is the joy one can die from.

It is the plunge that embraces comprehension and above all incomprehension.

It is magical, crude and graceful.

It is levitation and dreams in broad daylight.

It's mysterious and bewitching.

It is full and unintelligible.

It is the living and trembling nerve of what is today.

When it's within reach, behold, it's illusory because it continues being unreachable.

It is the enigma of nature.

It is parambolic –

whatever that word means.

My only salvation is happiness – the atonal happiness within the essential it.

Doesn't that make sense?

What do you mean when you say 'I?'

If I say 'I' it's because I don't dare say 'you' or 'we' or 'a person,' I am the you-are.

I'm behind thought.

I simply slip away, not leaving.

When I'm alive I tremble all over.

I'm not lying – my truth sparkles like the prism of a crystal chandelier.

Renouncing my name, I go beyond myself.

I don't want to ask why.

Ancient cockroaches drag themselves along in the half-light and all this am I, here I am, the cave and I, in the time that will rot us.

I have courage because of long suffering from the hell of love, but now I am heroic and I want the flowing.

I am before.

I am almost.

I am never.

I don't think just as the diamond doesn't think.

I let the freed horse run wildly.

I become full and unintelligible.

I'm the what.

I exceed my limits and only then do I exist and then in a feverish way.

God help me, I die so much.

I'm the centre of something that shouts and surges forth.

I know what I'm doing here – I'm counting the instances that drip and are thick with blood.

I know what I'm doing here, I'm improvising.

I go ahead intuitively without looking.

I exceed myself by abdicating myself and then I am the world.

I want the profound organic disorder that triggers the underlying order.

I don't like what I've just written but I'm forced to accept the whole passage because it happened to me and I respect very much what I cause to happen to myself.

What I do by involuntary instinct cannot be described.

Ugliness is my battle standard.

I delight in the difficult harmony of harsh contrasts.

Where am I going? The answer simply is: I'm going.

I'll make myself until I reach the core.

I'm ready to die and form many new compositions.

Sharp love, slow swoon, what I definitely am not is rationality.

I have a certain fear of myself, I'm not to be trusted, and I distrust my
    false power.

I'm not frightened anymore.

Let me speak, all right?

I have a deep anonymity, one that no one has ever touched.

What is there between never and always

that links them so indirectly and so intimately?

At the root of everything there's the hallelujah.

You who read me help me to be born.

Marvellous scandal

I is.

Thank you for taking the time from being dead.

YOU ARE

A WAY

OF BEING

ME

AND I

OF BEING

YOU

SHORT FILM III

SCENE ONE

In a large dance studio, a group of women are dancing.
The women dance to George Michael's 'Careless Whisper' –
their movements reminiscent of underwater plants –
clearly contemporary dance.

Each dancer a variation of quietly panicked effort.
The teacher is unseen but heard through her counting
and 'no' and 'feel it' and 'higher' and 'more' and 'right'
in an unforgiving voice.

Five shots of varying lengths (five to sixty seconds)
of the group dancing, and redancing,
to 'Careless Whisper.'

In each of these five shots, one dancer's memory
or body fails her and her face falters minutely just
as faces do upon accidental audible public flatulence.

The girl dances flawlessly to George Michael each time.

*Palette: Muted – beige of the wood floors, cool grey of the mirrors which
reflect the grey midday sky out the windows, grey, beige, black, and
pale pink clothes of the dancers. The pallor of the dancers also match
this sickly palette.*

SCENE TWO

The dancers sit, sweating and stretching, moderately so.
The camera is at their height – we see only the teacher's legs pacing
as she calls the names of the dancers who have made the company.
The dancers, who smile or go limp with relief, scurry off scene.
The girl, who has been sitting in the middle of the group, is called last.
Without expression, she too scurries off scene. The camera remains
on the group of disappointed dancers who just could not feel
'Careless Whisper' in a contemporary dance sort of way.
The teacher informs the chosen dancers they've a small break
before first rehearsal begins.

SCENE THREE

The girl is in the changeroom, at the bathroom sink.
The changeroom is a pink, an intrusive Pepto-Bismol pink.
She looks steadily into the mirror, into her own eyes.
She removes shaving cream and a razor, the faucet splashes.
The girl takes off her shirt – a thick carpet of hair
wraps from each shoulder, across her chest and belly
except for the perfect circles of her small breasts
which are hairless. She lathers her chest hair
and begins shaving diligently, though
with gravity and grace.

END SCENE.

A POSTHUMOUS INTERVIEW WITH W. G. SEBALD

INTRODUCTION

Sebald deals with the loss of personal and collective memory, with decay, seen through the wide lens of history. Sebald loves lists. Lists have a way of integrating and reconciling otherwise disparate things. Sebald's books are strung with nouns and proper nouns. By listing any array of things, one can't help noticing the connections between them. History is full of nouns. The nouns remain but the objects decay, the beads and combs and children's toys decay, the people decay, the empires and little families and old ways of doing things decay, our memories of them decay. By stringing the gone things together he resurrects them in their strangeness. Susan Sontag wondered if literary greatness was still possible after Sebald. Sebald understands space and time better than any physicist.

If a self is told linearly, is that self lying? Why does linear or chrono-logical narrative always seem to be a process of exclusion and simpli-fication? Even though it doesn't really resemble life, do we gravitate toward linear constructs for their order and simplicity? As a historian, why do you see no harm in blurring fact and fiction? Is history just storytelling? Why are your texts and your protagonists always walk-ing around? Why does it seem that your protagonists don't have any self but are instead an assemblage of multiple, interconnected narra-tives? I mean, who are you, Sebald?

The crocodile and the kangaroo, the anteater and the armadillo, the seahorse and the pelican; the chameleon and the salamander, the gryphon and the phoenix, the basilisk and the unicorn; the serpent with two heads and a mighty oak, a sow and a sausage, a piece of excrement and a field of clover, a white flower and a mulberry tree, a silk carpet –

The circumcision knives of Joshua, the ring which belonged to the mistress of Propertius, an ape of agate, a grasshopper, three-hundred golden bees, a blue opal, a silver belt buckle, a comb, an iron pin, a brass plate, a brazen nipper to pull away hair, and a brass jew's harp that last sounded on the crossing over the black water –

If we view ourselves from a great height, it is frightening to realize how little we know about our species, our purpose and our end; on every new thing there lies already the shadow of annihilation; in this continuous process of consuming and being consumed, nothing endures; all we wish for is to be forgotten, though an idiosyncracy peculiar to the herring is that, when dead, it begins to glow.

Can history be understood as a chronological sequence of events? Do things become comprehensible only when they are stacked properly? Or does this just make a skeleton? Is poetry translatable? Is calling yourself a historian similar to one who attempts to translate poetry in that it has to become something else? Is the only way to tell history to turn it into something else? What is your understanding of history in the first place?

It has a powerful tail fin, a narrow head, a slightly prominent lower mandible and a large eye, with a black pupil swimming in the silvery-white iris.

Why do I read your portrayal of history as a long song with a frequent refrain? Why does it make me think of time as some sort of cyclical, eternal return? To alter my previous question, if there is a song of history, what would you say it is, and what is its refrain?

Barley, malt, coffee, sugar beet syrup, cod-liver oil, torn sails of windmills, chests and tables, corpses rotting in the no man's land between the trenches, crates, feather beds, woodlands razed by artillery fire, firewood, straw and drowned livestock, gas stations, motels and shopping malls, mass slaughter in the swamps of Galicia, the sunlight and how it fell –

Nimrod is lost in Orion, and Osiris in the Dog Star. Pyramids, arches and obelisks are melting pillars of snow. Palaces and cloud-high towers collapse. Entire epochs pass in one awful second. Our history is but a long account of calamities possessed of a heart slowly reduced to embers.

St. Mary, St. Michael, St. Peter, St. James, St. Andrew, St. Lawrence, St. John; Philadelphia, New York, Boston, Brussels, Jersey, London, Milan, Verona, Venice, Rome, Naples, Vienna, Berlin, Potsdam, Constantinople, Jerusalem, Karlsbad, Prague and Pilsen, Bamberg, Versailles, Vichy and Paris; Jehovah's witnesses from Manchester, archeological experts from the Holy Land, ultra orthodox Jews from London and representatives of evangelist sects from California; the sunlight and how it fell –

Nimrod is lost in Orion, and Osiris in the Dog Star. Pyramids, arches and obelisks are melting pillars of snow. Palaces and cloud-high towers collapse. Entire epochs pass in one awful second. Our history is but a long account of calamities possessed of a heart slowly reduced to embers.

Huge oaks, ash and plane trees, beeches and limes, torn and mangled shrubs that had grown in their shade, thujas and yews, hazel and laurel bushes, holly and rhododendrons; never-ending streams of refugees, an arrangement of artificial twigs, colourful silk boys and tiny stuffed hummingbirds and a conical pile of china fruit; French towns reduced to rubble; curious handcart with a goose shut in a cage, dozens of windmills, timber, frost and adders, vipers and lizards of transparent ice, upended bathtubs and buckled heating pipes; the sunlight and how it fell –

Nimrod is lost in Orion, and Osiris in the Dog Star. Pyramids, arches and obelisks are melting pillars of snow. Palaces and cloud-high towers collapse. Entire epochs pass in one awful second. Our history is but a long account of calamities possessed of a heart slowly reduced to embers.

Battleships sinking under black clouds of petroleum smoke; salt, herring, wool and hides, bales and barrels, shattered cranes, derelict factories and zigzag rooftops, deadly nightshade, valerian, angelica and hot rhubarb; the Plough, the Tail of Draco, the Triangle of Taurus, the Pleiades, Pegasus, the Swan and the Dolphin; practical and ornamental horticulture, the urns found at Brampton in Norfolk, the making of artificial hills and burrows, the sunlight and how it fell –

Nimrod is lost in Orion, and Osiris in the Dog Star. Pyramids, arches and obelisks are melting pillars of snow. Palaces and cloud-high towers collapse. Entire epochs pass in one awful second. Our history is but a long account of calamities possessed of a heart slowly reduced to embers.

The several plants mentioned in Scripture, the Saxon tongue, the pronouncements of the Oracle at Delphi, the fishes eaten by our Saviour, the behaviour of the insects, hawks and falcons, and a case of Boulimia Centenaria which occurred in Yarmouth, a seascape with floating icebergs upon which sit walruses, bears, foxes and a variety of rare fowls, medals and coins, a precious stone from a vulture's head, a neat crucifix made out of a crossbone of a frog's head; the sunlight and how it fell –

Nimrod is lost in Orion, and Osiris in the Dog Star. Pyramids, arches and obelisks are melting pillars of snow. Palaces and cloud-high towers collapse. Entire epochs pass in one awful second. Our history is but a long account of calamities possessed of a heart slowly reduced to embers.

Ostrich and hummingbird eggs, bright-hued parakeet feathers, spirits and salt of Sargasso excellent against scurvy, marriageable ladies from the upper classes, silk brocades and watered tabinets, satins and satinettes, camblets and chevrettes, prunelles, callimancoes and florentines, diamantines and grenadines, blondines, bombazines, belle-isles and martiniques; from Riga to Rotterdam, from St. Petersburg to Seville, gnats wasps and flies – the sunlight and how it fell –

Such an emphasis on endings, but what about beginnings, especially in the context of an eternal recurrence? Are beginnings obsolete because they are already tainted with annihilation? In the conclusion to the Garden of Cyrus, Thomas Browne writes, 'All things began in order, so shall they end, and so shall they begin again'; What inspires your sense of eternal return?'

Across what distances do elective affinities and correspondences connect? 'For in and out, above, about, below, / 'Tis nothing but a magic shadow show, / Play'd in a box whose Candle is the sun, / Round which the phantom Figures come and go.' How is it that one perceives oneself in another human being, or, if not oneself, then one's own precursor?

Your sense of history is remarkably melancholic – does joy fit into this long account of calamities?

There are only two seasons: the white winter and the green winter. Scenes of destruction, mutilation, desecration, starvation, conflagration and freezing cold. However, I have always kept ducks – and the colour of their plumage, in particular the dark green and snow white, seemed to me the only possible answer to the questions that are on my mind.

A woman in her early thirties is shown performing all the rhythmic, banal things any human being does unselfconsciously throughout the day such as brushing teeth, tripping in legs of underwear, peeing, splashing water over her face, leaning on the counter while drinking orange juice out of the carton, staring into space combined with small disembodied shots such as her wrist wrenching the espresso filter handle, slipping her foot into her shoe, and so on.

The director has full creative licence over what banal tasks are shown, and in what sequence. However, there are four crucial things that must be included:

1. The film begins with the woman in bed, in the morning. She opens her eyes, stares for a solid, silent five seconds. Then cue the blaring sound of an air horn. The first blast should be sustained. It is important that the woman does not react to this sound. Instead, unblinking, she continues to stare, then rubs her eyes, stretches, rubs her face, gets out of bed and makes the bed. The air horn does stop intermittently, but only intermittently. Some blasts are brief, others not. Some silences are brief, others not. What is important is that she does not react to them.

2. The horn must blare in intervals throughout the entire film. The juxtaposition of what tasks the woman performs and horn-blast lengths are entirely up to the director. If choreographed well, a subtle humour should become apparent.

The director must treat the duration of this film as a psychological test. The ideal duration should be the amount of time it takes for half of the audience to leave.

Whatever the duration the film, enough time should be allotted to portray an even spectrum of an average day's activities and end with the final scene where:

3. The woman calmly slips into her tidy bed. She closes her eyes, the horn blares for a good ten seconds longer, then stops. The remaining audience members will be rewarded with a final thirty seconds of watching the woman sleep, the only sound being her breath.

4. The film is called *On Grief.* The title must be shown only at the end, when the final scene cuts out. The credits may be shown in silence, or maybe accompanied by music that no matter what – from Bach to the Beach Boys – will be absurd. Or, better, perhaps instead of music a sustained 'cheering stadium audience' track is played. Director's choice.

ON SEEING: AN INTERVIEW BETWEEN TWO SIDES OF ONE BRAIN, PERSONIFIED AS TWIN BROTHERS

INTRODUCTION

As science has ascertained, certain babies get hit on the head with a stone on their way down from the black hole and these babies are called empaths – a somewhat mystical deformity wherein the senses get both heightened and confused. The mix and amplitude and distortion of the empath's sensory experience varies from empath to empath. Empaths are best recognized due to their innate staring problem.

We, the babies who did not get hit on the head with a stone on our way down, have likely called the empaths names. They are easy targets because they don't fight back, or they do so in a baffling way wherein they wind up wounded by their own hand. We who did not get hit on the head with a stone might demand of the empaths, *Do you have a staring problem?* And the empaths will look over their own shoulders wondering who you are talking to, for empaths stare so hard their sense of physical body is totally erased and, as if they have no self, they become what it is they are looking at. They are surprised when others call them out as physical beings.

For them, it is not the name but the feeling of the name. For this reason, I decided to interview my twin brother, who is an empath. I used to call him many names, I often beat him up, and now I suffer from guilt and wish to know more of what goes on behind his disconcerting stare, since science has now ascertained that he got hit on the head with a stone on the way down while I didn't. What follows is a transcription of our interview.

Why do empaths have staring problems?

Sleeping is a way of staring. Sex is a way of staring. Taking off your socks is a way of staring. Opening your nostrils is a way of having your eyes open. Listening with your eyes closed is a way of staring. Crying comes with remarkable force and it too is a way of staring. Solitude is a way of staring at everything you picked up from the day and then solitude is for releasing it all as one shakes out a dusty mat over a railing because, as I said, sleeping is a way of staring and you have to prepare for that. I used to have night-terrors until I learned to shake off the day's staring. Night terrors means waking in the middle of the night screaming at the top of your lungs then promptly falling back asleep. Contrary to general assumption, being in a room of people is bad for staring – everyone's emotional information just blasts at me hard and unceasing – it is important to dumb down the senses in such situations, and here alcohol is one solution, the best being abstinence from such places.

With such an onslaught of sensory material, how do you make room for yourself, how do you define yourself?

My high school friend Candice was shy and and considered a nerd. At age twenty-five she started a charity and moved to Zambia and became a nurse. My ex-girlfriend's roommate Dion and his band mate Jeff, they are both dating lady-doctors [Liz and Meredith] and they are all only twenty-three. Geena Davis is an Olympic level archer. You became a banker, our parents are in love with God. Marie is a saint in the soul and has excellent taste and a rich boyfriend who flies her to New York City every weekend. Johnny has a rich father and two homes in B.C. Tom studies geology and squatted in New Orleans for a while and now he's in Toronto. There are conspiracy theorists, there are Marxists, there are moms. My friend Jess from high school became Christian, argued for creation versus evolution, and is now married with a baby – she posts about God on Facebook, she married her swim coach. Many of my friends from high school are married with children and houses – they run marathons and go on Pinterest. David Lynch loves the weather. Dawn's mom came out as a lesbian when Dawn was in high school. Once my friend Jeremy was just my normal friend Jeremy and now he has become famous – a number of my friends have also done so in variations. For example, modelling: Becka can go to Morocco for a week and get her pictures taken and make eighty thousand dollars. It has happened repeatedly where gunmen go into buildings and just start shooting. After Chris's mom died he bought a motorcycle, started eating meat and drove across the United States. My friend Alex is a single mom who over-works but being in her presence is definitely like being on a tropical beach – everything is turquoise, slower and more sexual. Men and women in my neighbourhood often walk under my window muttering things or screaming things in grave voices. Brad works for an IT company and hates it, he dreams about making music. June lives in Paris and has a very organized and radically inclined mind. Max had a nanny growing up, and so did Rena – both in Toronto – but didn't know each other. Viktor's uncle shot himself. Our dad had a pet crow. And our dad got his teeth punched out for not speaking French. Liz is never lacking money. Brenda lost her mind and lives in Texas. Georgia lost her mind. then got it back, then had a baby. That girl who used to flirt with me became a celebrated architect and stage designer and also has a health food Pinterest. I dunno. This is how I make room for myself. By pushing myself out.

I see you reading and studying all the time, you were always better than me in school, yet when you speak it's like you don't remember anything. Why?

Among the many things, I have extensively researched is the prison system in the United States of America, for example, and the information turns my brain into a blizzard of dead black animals of all sorts falling from the sky turning everything that was once distinguishable into dark matter. Of course if you asked me for facts about the prison system I couldn't give you any, but I know the best way to articulate the whole ordeal is to fall down in a seizure right here in front of you. I'm whirled and drowned in maelstroms of rhododendrons! Full flowers! Round eyes! Rush upward! Rapture! Space!

How are you with the girls?

Girls have gotten jealous because I am as interested in dead leaves on the sidewalk as much as I am interested in them. Even pylons fascinate me. When partners are gone from my bed I do not notice because the presence of the sheets and the mattress below me and the feel of the room, and maybe the breeze, if there is a window, feels just like a lover but a gentler one, and less demanding. I feel like everyone is my sweetheart and I don't even need them to touch me or talk to me. I prefer to watch them do the things they do to each other, sometimes with horror, though I do often feel left out but wouldn't have it any other way. How is it that one can never do enough for one's mother? All the world's tulips would just be excessive, yet still hardly enough. Growing up, I'd never notice a mess until you saw it – otherwise I was one with it. I sleep beneath a mountain of books but nothing remains distinct in my brain so my mind is this syrupy swamp water but I don't know – if you swam around in there it is probably mineral-rich and makes your skin soft or you might get a rash or you might drown, I don't know. I know people are doing things in all the downtown buildings, but I cannot fathom what, or how, or why. New York is paralyzing. My dream job is to be a keeper of sheep but I have no idea how to get there.

Can you tell time?

I get fired from all my jobs because I am so happy to just walk along and listen to so much music but never remember the name of it – it all just moves right through me and I experience it but I do not want to hold on to any of it; I am basically already dead, empaths are friendly ghosts and we will never remember your name – so yeah, I just forget to go to work on the way there. While it is a problem that my brain lacks any organization whatsoever I also intuit that it may be a great freedom. Some people remember everything – they are the ones with their feet on the ground, they will be the ones who are celebrated and win awards and cure diseases, and we are the ones with our feet firmly and decidedly off the ground because science has now proven we got hit on the head with a stone on our way down. I've spent hours in galleries and looking at books of art and artists and I cannot remember any name or date at all but the experience was always as wonderful as I could ever wish an experience to be. When people gossip about me I wonder who they are talking about – the words are neon pink and blare like an air-strike warning and I fall to my knees and cover my head. I've read Paul Bowles and Wittgenstein and Doris Lessing and Dorothy Parker and Basho and Celan and O'Hara and maybe four hundred or four thousand more and I couldn't tell you a thing about them except they each offered an experience and that's it. My feelings are always both hurt and elated. I am amazed at how so many people work to make the world appear solid, or that their world may in fact be solid. All the things in the dollar store, all those key chains that are squishy plastic little pigs – a lot of work went into getting those to the till at the Dollarama in Montreal. It dazzles me and I stare. People have all these opinions and ideas and I just listen. I watch them have ambitions. That's all I can say on the matter, I'd rather we hold hands and say nothing at all.

Each season is three minutes and six seconds long which is the exact duration of Glenn Gould's 'Aria,' a variation of Bach's 'Aria Da Capo.' The song repeats in its entirety for each season.

Spring, 'Aria' begins: The girl in a trench coat stands at the corner of Notre Dame and Charlevoix, waiting at a red light, staring fixedly at the red light. The light does not change. The 'Aria' is in no hurry.

[In the background, it is spring. Spring foliage, spring things. A couple dressed for spring, holding coffees, walk their dog who pees on the post next to the girl. A homeless man, too, has a spring to his step – he doesn't ask anyone for anything. The sky darkens, and for the last minute of the 'Aria,' it begins pouring. The girl remains still and gets rained on while the people behind her run for shelter or walk swiftly and purposefully in step, umbrellas in hand. The girl flips her collar. The light is still red. End scene, 'Aria' ends.]

Summer, 'Aria' begins: The girl in a slightly dirtier trench coat is still standing at the corner of Notre Dame and Charlevoix, waiting at a red light and staring fixedly at the red light. The light does not change. The 'Aria' is in no hurry.

[In the background is a repetition of the spring things, but this time it is summer things and summer people and summer foliage. The homeless person this time is topless and asks the girl for money; she ignores him and her gaze never leaves the red light. The dog's tongue dangles, the dog tries to pee at the post though nothing comes out, its owners drink iced coffees and wear sandals, etc. Near the end of the 'Aria,' the girl tries to blow a loose, wet hair off her forehead. Her cheeks are flushed and rivulets of sweat run down her temples. The light is still red. End scene, 'Aria' ends.]

Fall, 'Aria' begins: The girl in a worn trench coat is still standing at the corner of Notre Dame and Charlevoix, waiting at a red light, and staring fixedly at the red light. The light does not change. The 'Aria' is in no hurry.

[In the background, fall things, fall foliage. This time the homeless person wears a toque and follows the couple with the dog who pees at the post asking them for money, hand outstretched. Near the end of the 'Aria,' the girl pulls her trench coat closer to her body, and a wind-carried leaf flies onto her face. She does not remove it. The light is still red. End scene, 'Aria' ends.]

Winter, 'Aria' begins: The girl stands at the corner of Notre Dame and Charlevoix, waiting at a red light, and staring fixedly at the red light. The light does not change. The 'Aria' is in no hurry.

[In the background, winter things. The couple rushes by, and they yank the dog as he tries to pee on the post. The homeless man is bundled and begs the unmoving girl for money. Eventually, he gives up and walks away. Her hair, eyelashes and shoulders are coated in snow. She is shivering. The light is still red. End scene, 'Aria' ends.]

Spring, 'Aria' begins: the girl stands at the corner of Notre Dame and Charlevoix, waiting at a red light, and staring fixedly at the red light. The 'Aria' abruptly stops. The light turns green, and the girl, without a change in facial expression, though much thinner in her markedly filthy coat, crosses the street.

ACKNOWLEDGEMENTS

Thank you to: Canada Council for the Arts for making the first draft of this book possible, even though I had proposed a completely different roject // My family for being supportive against all reason // Stephen for being the steadiest beacon of friendship, generosity and care, for being a rock, for keeping me together the last seven years, for without you I surely would have been eaten by the dingos and dringuses // My friends – supportive, kind, outstanding, impressive, intelligent, ever-weird – I'm in love // My enemies, for keeping it Real // Drawn and Quarterly for doling out previous LB books to the masses and for all you do for the literary community // Myriade Coffee because you fuel me and give me stomach-rot of gourmet proportions // Huck because you are Pip's friend // The various wonderful publications that have published much earlier drafts of some of these poems // Cam for reminding me I know nothing of the *Tao Te Ching* and for an early editing just out of the kindness of your heart // Sari for the name and Matt for helping refine the name of this book // Metatron for being you, and for turning the first version of 'Interviews' into one of your gorgeous publications // Weirdo for a daily example of what being one with the Way looks like and for being a blob // Jeramy and Coach House Books for making this book possible – it is an honour.

If you walk into the line of fire, you will be shot; when you are shot, that wound hardens into a trauma, a ghost wound that only you feel and perhaps act out on symptomatically to the confusion of those around you. A traumatic experience becomes a ghost wound becomes a recurring dream, and in the case of these Short Films, the recurring dream is extracted from the mind and turned into a 'short film.' All things become other things, this is that.

By a trauma involuntarily turning into a recurring dream, and thereby voluntarily turning the dream into a short film, it is an attempt at transmutation (the oneiric dream form materializes on the page in 'film form') and also an attempt at alchemy (the recurring dream, by being pulled from the unconscious and onto the page, ceases being a recurring dream, ceases being tyrannical, and instead becomes something odd yet innocuous when observed outside the self). Perhaps *alchemy* is too gentle a term when the word is *exorcism*, since the attempt is to excise the ghost wound so that the flesh may be rendered back to its pliant, healthy state of everyday skin, skin that is indeed susceptible to bacteria and blemishes and burns, but flesh as it is in all of its fleshiness rather than suffering from a psychosomatic bullet wound that refuses to close.

While dream forms never resemble the actual trauma forms, their content does – typical stuff like finding oneself in a compromised position, experiencing overwhelming desperation, calling to a loved one who cannot or will not hear you, trying to scream but finding you have no voice – or the inverse, finding you cannot stop screaming, being humiliated in the eyes of others, enacting violent feelings, paralyzation, and so on. Film form is formed around dream content.

You might notice that each film emphasizes that the actress is pretty, young and in good shape (and of course it goes without saying that she is white). This is because in the law of Hollywood, a conventionally unattractive woman will be perceived as all the more unattractive if the unattractive woman is experiencing unattractive emotions or if she is placed in a compromising position – such a woman in such a situation does not merit pathos, so sayeth the cultural laws, and such a woman in such a situation will surely make viewers turn away from her, such an insult she is to our sensibilities, so sayeth the law. A conventionally attractive woman however has more hope and leverage in that people will be less inclined to look away if she finds herself feeling unattractive emotions (while looking very attractive) or acting most unpleasant (while looking most attractive). The law of Hollywood does not apply to male leads, for if their looks are as complexly unpleasant as their inner worlds, they are all the more compelling.

Hollywood has a way of insulting subtlety to its very core; take for example the Hollywood adaptation of Gillian Flynn's *Gone Girl* in which the female lead is permitted a level of evil complexity not often shown, yet when her evil is revealed, she immediately allows herself to gain a huge amount of weight and stop wearing makeup not only to disguise herself while in hiding, but also to show in no subtle way that in Hollywood, physical unattractiveness is implicitly synonymous with evil and excess, especially when it comes to women. In Hollywood law, the language for a woman's emotional range is archaic, anything dipping below neutral being dismissed as 'bitchy,' 'crazy,' 'evil' and 'hysterical,' or any combination of the four, while their male contemporaries are provided with a vast vocabulary for their troubled minds and emotional landscapes because we want to look deeper into the unattractive male's complicated psyche to find the underlying reason that is undoubtedly there. The latter is met with fascination while the former is met with revulsion. If people look away from my female lead, what hope does she have to be saved? She may be demonized and humiliated, isolated and desperate, but she loves Pilates.

While Hollywood is base, dreams are camp by nature (no surprise that many of David Lynch's films come from dreams), they are bizarre without any explanation, they are grindingly repetitive, they are infused with anxiety, and the combination of these things often result in a gallows humour and absurdity that frees the dreamer from the grip of raw emotion once the dreamer sees it projected on a screen outside of the dream.

LAURA BROADBENT is the author of *Oh There You Are I Can't See You Is It Raining?*, which won the 2012 Robert Kroetsch Award for Innovative Poetry. She lives in Montreal.

Typeset in Laurentian, a typeface designed by Rod McDonald in 2003 for *Maclean's* magazine. McDonald took influence from the fonts designed by Claude Garamond and William Caslon and gave his alphabet a strong vertical stress, high x-height and narrow proportions.

Printed at the Coach House on bpNichol Lane in Toronto, Ontario, on Zephyr Antique Laid paper, which was manufactured, acid-free, in Saint-Jérôme, Quebec, from second-growth forests. This book was printed with vegetable-based ink on a 1965 Heidelberg KORD offset litho press. Its pages were folded on a Baumfolder, gathered by hand, bound on a Sulby Auto-Minabinda and trimmed on a Polar single-knife cutter.

Edited by Jeramy Dodds
Designed by Taylor Berry
Cover design by Natalie Olsen
Author photo by Rebecca Storm

Coach House Books
80 bpNichol Lane
Toronto ON M5S 3J4
Canada

416 979 2217
800 367 6360

mail@chbooks.com
www.chbooks.com